New York Cookbook

Barbara Bloch

ILLUSTRATED BY SUSAN DAVID

• • • • •

First published in 1991 by
The Appletree Press Ltd
14 Howard Street South
Belfast BT7 1AP
Tel:+44 (0) 28 90 243074
Fax:+44 (0) 28 90 246756
E-mail: reception@appletree.ie
Web Site:www.appletree.ie

A Little New York Cookbook

First published in the United States in 1991 by
Chronicle Books LLC, 85 Second Street,
San Francisco, California 94105

ISBN 0-87701-876-6

9 8 7 6 5 4

Introduction

Much to my surprise, even though I was born and raised in New York City, and have always lived close to it, I found it difficult to define New York City food. Much of the food that gained fame in New York is now available throughout the country and is no longer unique to the city. And, although the history of New York food includes world-famous dishes created by talented chefs for the elegant dining rooms of Delmonico's and the Ritz Carleton (and more broadly popular places like Lindy's, famous for its cheesecake), few modern chefs have gained fame for recent specific creations.

However, even if few specific foods accurately symbolize the city, there are some types of food special to New York. "Deli" food has been honed to a fine art and can be found in famous restaurants and equally famous food stores where you can find never-to-be-forgotten sandwiches or buy an unbelievable assortment of "deli" foods. Street food, ranging from frankfurters to felafel, is an integral part of the cuisine in New York, one of the few cities to allow the sale of cooked foods from pushcarts. Dishes made famous at such renowned New York restaurants as Delmonico's have set a trend for public eating in America as well as contributed to the development of American cuisine. And finally, almost every ethnic food, simple or elegant, can be found somewhere in the city. You can probably find whatever kind of food you want in New York if you look hard enough. The city can truthfully boast that it is the ethnic food capital of the world.

A note on measures   Spoon and dry cup measurements are level. Seasonings can of course be adjusted to taste. Recipes are for four unless otherwise indicated.

Vichyssoise

This soup, with the very French name, is an American version of French Leek and Potato Soup, and was created by Chef Louis Diat at the Ritz Carleton Hotel in 1910. He substituted scallions for leeks and served the soup cold instead of hot. You can use either leeks or scallions, but the soup must be very thick, very creamy, and very well chilled.

---

3 tbsp butter
4 leeks (white part only), thoroughly washed and sliced
4 medium-size potatoes, peeled and diced
4 cups well-flavored chicken stock
2 cups half and half or milk
salt and white pepper to taste
about 1 cup heavy cream
freshly snipped chives to garnish
(serves 6)

Melt butter in saucepan, add leeks, and sauté until softened. Add potatoes and chicken stock, cover, and cook 25 minutes or until potatoes are very tender. Purée in 2 or 3 batches in food processor or blender. Return to saucepan, stir in half and half, and season to taste. Simmer 5 minutes. Refrigerate several hours or until thoroughly chilled. Beat in heavy cream, increasing or decreasing amount as necessary to keep soup thick. Ladle into small serving bowls and garnish with snipped chives.

Manhattan Clam Chowder

The original New England Clam Chowder was made with milk and cream, never tomatoes. When the good citizens of Rhode Island (and some say Connecticut as well) substituted tomatoes for milk and cream, the reaction of other New Englanders was utter scorn. And, even though New Yorkers had nothing to do with this "heresy," there were those who were certain only New Yorkers could be responsible for such "bad taste." One must conclude that calling this soup "Manhattan" Clam Chowder was not exactly meant as a compliment. No matter. We can be proud to claim it, provided it's properly made with crisp vegetables. This can be a delicious soup.

---

¹/₄ lb salt pork, finely chopped
I onion and I small green pepper, chopped
2 dozen littleneck or cherrystone clams, steamed and chopped,
broth reserved and thoroughly strained
bottled clam juice
4 large tomatoes, peeled and diced
¹/₂ tsp each thyme and salt
hot pepper sauce to taste
3 potatoes and 3 carrots, peeled and cubed

Sauté pork in large saucepan. Add onion and pepper and cook until softened. Measure clam broth and add enough clam juice to make 5 cups. Add to saucepan with tomatoes and seasonings. Simmer 10 minutes. Add potatoes and cook 10 minutes. Add carrots and clams and cook 10 minutes or until vegetables are just tender.

Waldorf Salad

Great restaurants like Delmonico's, with talented chefs in their kitchens, are remembered for many fine dishes. But the famous Oscar Tschirky of the Waldorf is remembered for only one — Waldorf Salad. He was not a chef and there are some who are not at all certain he created the salad. Oscar originally worked at Delmonico's and his considerable talent was not in cooking but as a maître d'hôtel. There's no argument, however, about the fact that it was he who made the dining room at the Waldorf one of the finest in the country shortly before the turn of the century. The original recipe for Waldorf Salad did not include walnuts. They appeared about twenty years after the salad was first created and have become a standard part of the recipe.

---

2 large, firm apples, cored and cut into large dice
lemon juice
2 large stalks celery, diced
³/₄ cup chopped walnuts
2 tbsp light or heavy cream (optional)
²/₃ cup mayonnaise
Boston lettuce to serve

Place unpeeled apples in bowl and sprinkle with lemon juice. Add celery and walnuts. Stir cream into mayonnaise, add to apple mixture, and toss gently. Arrange lettuce on salad plates and spoon salad onto lettuce.

America's Best-Known Restaurant – Delmonico's

Arguably, the original Delmonico's was the most famous restaurant in America. It opened in lower Manhattan in 1831 and within a short time revolutionized public eating in America. The only restaurant still in existence in New York older than Delmonico's is Fraunces Tavern where George Washington bade farewell to his officers in 1783. But Samuel Fraunces didn't have the impact on American eating habits, or New York society, that the Delmonico brothers had. Elegant, stylish, opulent, and spotlessly clean (unusual for that period), Delmonico's offered fresh food, cooked in the French manner, served by a staff of attentive waiters. Everything about Delmonico's was new to America.

Patrons included every president from Monroe to F.D.R. Dickens was feted there and Thackeray complained about the prices, but continued to eat there anyway. Diamond Jim Brady and Lillian Russell were regular customers. It was the "in" place for all of New York society.

Many dishes made famous at Delmonico's have become part of the lexicon of American food. Delmonico Steak, Lobster Newburg, and Delmonico Potatoes are among the best known.

Delmonico Steak Is not a recipe; it's a cut of meat. Now that meat cuts have standardized names you can duplicate it easily. Buy a thick, boneless rib eye steak, season with freshly ground pepper, and broil to desired doneness.

Lobster Newburg

This famous recipe was brought to Delmonico's by Ben Wenberg, a sea captain who was a regular customer. Charles Delmonico was so delighted he named the dish Lobster à la Wenberg. Eventually Wenberg and Delmonico had a falling-out and, in anger, Delmonico renamed the dish Newberg by reversing the first and third letters. Over the years Newberg changed through misspelling to Newburg, the name still used for this dish throughout the world.

---

3 egg yolks
1 1/2 cups heavy cream
cayenne, salt, and freshly ground pepper to taste
2 1/2 cups cooked, sliced lobster meat
2 to 3 tbsp Madeira, dry sherry, or Cognac
1 tbsp butter
cooked rice ring to serve
freshly chopped parsley to garnish
(serves 4 to 6)

Beat egg yolks in top of double boiler off heat. Add cream and beat until well combined. Place pan over (not in) simmering water and cook, stirring, until mixture is thick enough to coat spoon. Add seasonings and stir in lobster meat. Cook gently until lobster is heated through. Stir in Madeira and butter. Spoon into center of rice ring and garnish with parsley.

Delmonico Potatoes

There is no recipe called Delmonico Potatoes in the old cookbook of Delmonico's Chef Charles Ranhofer. But there is a recipe for creamed potatoes that approximates the recipe below, a dish generally thought of as Delmonico Potatoes.

---

3 tbsp each butter and all-purpose flour
1 1/2 cups half and half
salt and freshly ground pepper to taste
6 medium-size potatoes, cooked, peeled, and cubed
3/4 cup grated sharp Cheddar or Swiss cheese
dry bread crumbs

Preheat oven to 375°F. Melt butter in saucepan, stir in flour, and cook 2 minutes. Add cream slowly, stirring constantly, and cook until thickened. Season and stir in potatoes. Layer half of potatoes in buttered baking dish and top with half of cheese. Repeat layers and sprinkle with bread crumbs. Bake 25 to 30 minutes.

The 1923 closing of the original Delmonico's was the result of Prohibition. Unwilling to become an illegal speakeasy, Delmonico's served liquor openly and eventually was raided. Financial ruin followed. In 1982 Delmonico's was reopened by new owners at the old location and every effort was made to duplicate the decor of the original, using old photographs. However, since America's eating habits have changed, the incredible opulent feasts of the past are no longer served.

Soda Fountain Nostalgia

Ask people to name food typical of New York and, even if they only come up with one, they're sure to name Egg Creams. But finding an Egg Cream in the city today is like looking for a needle in a haystack. They used to be sold at the corner soda fountain, but corner soda fountains are no more. Egg Cream is something of a misnomer since there are no eggs in the drink. When you can find them they're made with equal amounts of vanilla or chocolate syrup and very cold milk into which a hard stream of seltzer is squirted to create a foamy top that looks like beaten egg whites, something that cannot be duplicated at home with a bottle of seltzer. Every so often an Egg Cream does pop up on a store sign or menu, but not very frequently.

When I was growing up in the city, the best treat anyone could offer me was a trip to Schrafft's, a chain of restaurants that no longer exists. In the back of each Schrafft's were tables where "ladies lunched" on watercress sandwiches. But in the front there was a long, elegant soda fountain where grandparents brought their grandchildren, often at a time of day when no responsible parent would have allowed a child to have ice cream. I always ordered a Hot Butterscotch Sundae: two enormous scoops of coffee ice cream, covered with hot butterscotch sauce, topped with large, salty almonds, a huge mound of whipped cream, and a cherry. It was the ambrosia of my childhood, something no present-day ice cream parlor has ever equaled.

"Street Food" in the Big Apple

To see vendors selling food from pushcarts is not unusual in Europe, but it's rare in America. New York City is one of the few cities that permit it. There are only two kinds of food expressly prohibited for sale by the health department — raw shellfish and sushi. As a result, a remarkable variety of food is available. Some of the food is seasonal; hot chestnuts in winter, ice cream and Sno-Cones or Italian fruit-flavored ices in summer. Some foods, like Chinese Egg Rolls, are pretty much, although not entirely, confined to ethnic areas of the city. But in midtown Manhattan, year 'round, there's a wide selection of food sold from pushcarts where a surprising number of midtown office workers buy their lunches, taking the food back to their offices in cold or rainy weather, and eating it out-of-doors in nice weather.

Some of the food sold is standard and unexciting: nuts, candy, soda, popcorn, potato chips, pizza, cookies, Danish pastry, and of course, pretzels, salty or plain. Frankfurters are available everywhere, covered with hot sauerkraut if you wish. A variety of other kinds of sausage is also available, with or without peppers, as are tacos with all kinds of fillings, and chili, hot or mild. What is surprising is the number of Middle Eastern foods, Arabic and kosher, sold side by side. The food they sell is similar even to the point that, in many cases, neither sell pork. Typically you can find Felafel, Gyros, Kofta and Shish Kebabs, Knishes, Souvlaki, Shwarma, and Babaganouj, many of them served in pita pockets with a variety of condiments, sauces, and shredded lettuce or other salad foods.

Felafel: Deep-fried balls made with mashed chick-peas and bulgar, served with tachina (sesame sauce).

Gyros: Shaved slices of ground, pressed loaves of meat, usually lamb, cooked on a spit, served in pita pockets with yogurt sauce and salad.

Kofta Kebabs: Sausage-shaped ground meat cooked on a skewer.

Shish Kebabs: Standard combination of meat and vegetables cooked on a skewer over a grill.

Knishes: Unsweetened pastry filled with potatoes, cheese, or meat.

Souvlaki: Similar to Shish Kebabs, but with different seasoning.

Shwarma: Meat loaf, cooked on a spit.

Babaganouj: Cooked, mashed eggplant seasoned with tachina.

Kofta Kebabs

2 lb ground lamb or beef (or 1 lb each)
2 eggs, beaten
2 onions, minced
$1/2$ tsp each coriander and cumin
cayenne, salt, and freshly ground pepper to taste
pita bread to serve

Combine all ingredients except pita bread and mix well. Form into small sausage-shapes around flat-edge skewers. Cook over charcoal, turning often to brown and crisp on all sides. Serve in pita pockets.

If desired, kebab vegetables such as wedges of eggplant,

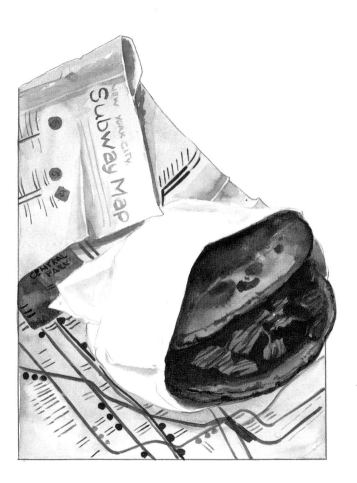

mushrooms, cocktail tomatoes, and small onions can be cooked on separate skewers and served with Kofta Kebabs.

Babaganouj

1 eggplant, about 1 lb
1 clove garlic, crushed
4 tbsp lemon juice
3 tbsp tachina (sesame sauce)
salt to taste
1 tbsp olive oil
pita bread to serve
1 small onion, finely chopped and freshly
chopped parsley to garnish

Preheat oven to 375°F. Prick eggplant with fork several times, place on baking sheet, and bake about 45 minutes or until tender. When cool enough to handle, peel and mash. Stir in garlic, lemon juice, tachina, and salt. Sprinkle with olive oil and serve in pita pockets, garnished with onion and parsley.

New York Delicatessens

The word "delicatessen" comes to us from the German word "delikatesse" meaning delicacy. And there is no doubt a good delicatessen will have an incredible array of delicacies to offer. The first delicatessens appear to have opened in America around 1880. They were Jewish shops, some kosher and some not, that sold food best described as Jewish delicacies. Although this is still true in most instances, many delicatessens have expanded their stock to include other ethnic foods and, in certain neighborhoods, a food as basic as good Jewish rye bread cannot be found because the food sold is almost entirely Italian.

New York City has the usual neighborhood and supermarket delicatessens found in many cities, some excellent and some not worth going into. The city also has some of the best delicatessens in the world. You'll find two very different kinds of special delicatessens. Some are famous restaurants like the Carnegie or Stage Delicatessen where, although they also sell food to take home, it's mostly sandwiches and desserts. And then there's Zabar's, a food store like no other in the world, where the choice of foods you can buy is overwhleming and will leave you almost breathless.

Eating in a Delicatessen

Delicatessen eating is likely to be a very social affair. Your waiter will probably have an opinion about your order, and feel no hesitancy about expressing it. The more critical he is, the more likely he is to say something. Your neighbor is likely to express his opinion too. At first glance you may think the restaurant is kosher. Jewish food predominates. But, if you check, you'll also find several kinds of ham, bacon in the turkey sandwich, and shrimp in a salad or sandwich.

You can start your meal with herring, chopped liver, sturgeon, gefilte fish, chicken soup with matzo balls or kreplach, or borscht, hot or cold. But, if you're going to order a sandwich, don't eat too much first. Some delicatessens claim there is $3/4$ lb of meat in each sandwich and it may be true. I've never weighed the meat, but I'm certain there's at least $1/2$ lb, and it's assumed you'll probably ask for a doggy bag. Sandwiches include the best pastrami or corned beef, hot or cold, you can find anywhere, served on superb rye bread or pumpernickel. You can order sandwiches with three kinds of meat in the same sandwich or you can choose standards like smoked salmon (lox) and cream cheese on a bagel, triple-decker turkey, ham, and cheese, or a Reuben sandwich (page 28). There are side dishes of creamy coleslaw (page 31), French fried potatoes, latkes, fried onion rings, baked beans, or sauerkraut. There is a whole selection of omelettes, fried chicken, full dinners, and lots of salads. And then there are desserts — Cheesecake (page 31), 7-layer cake, strudel, cream pies, fruit pies, strawberry short cake, fresh fruit, ice cream, and more. And most of the food is superb.

Reuben Sandwich

Craig Claiborne must be credited for his efforts to research the origin of the Reuben Sandwich. He unearthed two versions. One version credits the winner of a National Sandwich Contest in 1956 for submitting a recipe she got from a friend of her father whose name was "Reuben" Kay. The other version credits Arnold "Reuben," owner of Reuben's Restaurant in New York City for inventing the sandwich in 1914. Although the second version seems to be the one most people have always assumed to be correct, Mr. Claiborne considers the first version the more credible. In whatever way this sandwich came to be, it's great eating.

Per sandwich:
1 large slice pumpernickel or rye bread
Russian dressing
4 to 6 slices corned beef, thinly sliced
enough thoroughly drained sauerkraut to cover meat
2 or 3 slices imported Swiss cheese
pickles to serve

Spread bread with Russian dressing, top with corned beef, sauerkraut, and then cheese. Place in broiler, several inches from source of heat, and cook just until cheese is melted and lightly browned on top. Serve with pickles.

New York Cole Slaw

---

¹/₂ cup each mayonnaise and dairy sour cream
2 tbsp each Dijon-style mustard and tarragon vinegar
I tsp sugar
salt and freshly ground pepper to taste
I head cabbage (about I lb), shredded

Combine all ingredients except cabbage and mix well. Toss with cabbage. Refrigerate and serve chilled.

No-Bake Cheesecake

Lindy's, famous for their cheesecake, closed in 1969. This recipe is unique because it does NOT claim to be their recipe!

Crust:
12 graham crackers, crushed
2 tbsp sugar
4 tbsp butter, melted
Filling:
2 pkgs (¹/₄ oz each) unflavored gelatin
3 egg yolks
²/₃ cup sugar
I cup small curd cottage cheese
I pkg (8oz) cream cheese
juice and grated peel of I large lemon
I tsp vanilla
2 cups dairy sour cream
fresh berries to decorate

Grease 8-inch springform pan. Mix graham cracker crumbs and sugar in small bowl. Add melted butter and stir until well combined. Press evenly onto bottom of prepared pan. Place in freezer at least 10 minutes to set. Sprinkle gelatin over 4 tbsp cold water, stir, and set aside. Place egg yolks and sugar in top of double boiler and beat until thickened and lemon colored. Place pan over (not in) simmering water and cook, stirring, until sugar is dissolved. Stir in gelatin and cook, stirring, until gelatin is dissolved and mixture is thickened. Remove from heat and cool completely. Place cottage cheese and cream cheese in large bowl and beat until almost smooth. Stir in lemon juice, lemon peel, and vanilla. Add cooled gelatin mixture gradually and beat until well combined. Stir in sour cream. Pour over crust, smooth top, and refrigerate at least 4 hours or until set. When ready to serve, run sharp knife around inside edge of pan before releasing side of pan. Place on serving plate without removing bottom of pan. Decorate with fresh berries.

Note: In place of lemon juice and lemon peel, substitute any of the following: orange juice and orange peel; 1 tbsp instant coffee dissolved in 1 tbsp hot water; 2 or 3 tbsp brandy. If desired, spread flavored whipped cream on top of cheesecake before adding berries.

Delicatessen Shopping

Of all the delicatessens in the world, it's not likely you can find one anywhere equal to Zabar's. It's a New York treasure. Speaking in round figures, and subject to change, they sell: approximately 400 kinds of cheese; 25 varieties of salami; 35 choices of ham; 20 kinds of wurst; more than 50 additional cold cuts; 25 different pates; over 10 kinds of smoked salmon; about 20 other varieties of smoked fish; at least 5 kinds of caviar; 40 different kinds of breads and rolls; about 40 varieties of beer and ale from more than 18 countries; 25 different coffees and teas; more than 20 desserts; fresh pastas; salads; cooked foods; olives; pickles; relishes; chocolate; and on, and on, and on. If you want to learn about the kind of food available in New York City, there's no better place to go than Zabar's.

Caviar Dip

1 pkg (3 oz) cream cheese, softened
1 cup dairy sour cream
1 jar (2 oz) red salmon caviar
2 tsp grated onion
1 tsp fresh lemon juice
crudités to serve

Combine cream cheese and sour cream. Stir in caviar, onion, and lemon juice. Chill well and serve with crudités.

Brunch in The Big Apple

Sunday is brunch time in New York. Hotels offer elegant buffet tables, and neighborhood restaurants serve fancier-than-usual breakfast and lunch dishes for late sleepers and hungry joggers. Brunch at home is a popular way to entertain, usually less formal and complicated than a dinner party. Both of the following recipes are great for brunch.

Spinach Soufflé

butter and freshly grated Parmesan cheese
3 1/2 tbsp butter
4 1/2 tbsp all-purpose flour
1 1/2 cups milk
6 egg yolks
1 pkg (10 oz) frozen chopped spinach, cooked and drained
nutmeg, hot pepper sauce, and salt to taste
7 egg whites
(serves 6)

Preheat oven to 400°F. Butter inside of 2-quart soufflé dish and sprinkle with cheese. Melt butter in saucepan, stir in flour, and cook 2 minutes. Add milk slowly, stirring constantly. Cook until thickened. Remove from heat and add egg yolks, 1 at a time, beating constantly. Purée spinach and stir into mixture. Season. Beat egg whites until stiff peaks form. Fold into spinach mixture and turn into souffle dish. Place in oven, reduce heat to 375°F, and bake about 30 minutes or until well

risen and lightly browned on top. Serve immediately with hot breakfast sausages and warm croissants.

Big Apple Crêpes

1 1/2 cups milk
3 eggs
3 tbsp Calvados
1 cup plus 2 tbsp all-purpose flour
4 tbsp superfine sugar
1/4 tsp salt
5 tbsp melted sweet butter plus butter for cooking
about 5 medium-size firm apples, peeled and diced
5 tbsp granulated sugar
confectioners sugar to serve
(makes about 18 crêpes)

Combine first 7 ingredients in blender in order given above. Process until well combined. Pour into pitcher, cover, and refrigerate at least 2 hours or overnight. Stir batter before using and add additional milk, if necessary, to make batter consistency of light cream. Melt 1/2 tsp butter in 7-inch crêpe pan. Make crêpe and keep warm. Repeat. Melt 4 tbsp butter in large skillet. Add apples, sprinkle with granulated sugar, and sauté, stirring, until lightly browned but still firm. Place 2 tbsp cooked apple on each crêpe and roll. Arrange 3 filled, warm crêpes on serving plate, seam side down, and dust with confectioners' sugar.

Long Island Duckling
with Raspberry Sauce

The first ducks arrived in New York from China in 1873. The descendants of those four ducks now constitute half of the ducks produced as food in America!

---

2 ducklings, about 4 1/2 lb each
salt and freshly ground pepper
2 pkgs (10 oz each) frozen raspberries, thawed
1/2 cup sugar
2 tbsp cornstarch
1 cup dry white wine
2 tbsp lemon juice
1/2 cup red currant jelly
4 tbsp raspberry or orange-flavored liqueur
fresh raspberries to garnish (optional)
(serves 6)

Preheat oven to 350°F. Cut ducks into serving-size pieces. Season with salt and pepper, prick all over with fork, place on rack in roasting pan, and bake about 2 hours or until very crisp. Drain liquid from raspberries and reserve. Mash berries and set aside. Place sugar and cornstarch in saucepan and mix. Stir in reserved berry liquid, wine, and lemon juice. Add jelly and cook, stirring, until jelly has melted and sauce begins to thicken. Add liqueur and mashed berries and cook until heated through. Place duck on serving platter, spoon some sauce over, and garnish with fresh berries. Serve remaining sauce separately.

Scalloped Oysters

Fresh seafood is available all over the city. Areas like City Island in the Bronx have seafood restaurants end to end. One of the most famous (and expensive) seafood restaurants in the city is a recently renovated landmark in Grand Central Station, The Grand Central Oyster Bar and Restaurant. It's not unusual for them to have about fifteen varieties of oysters on their menu.

---

^{1}/$_2$ cup butter
20 soda crackers, crushed
1 cup dry bread crumbs
salt and freshly ground pepper to taste
24 fresh oysters, shucked, liquor reserved
about ^{3}/$_4$ cup light cream
^{1}/$_4$ tsp Worcestershire sauce
hot pepper sauce to taste

Preheat oven to 350°F. Melt butter in skillet. Stir In crushed crackers, bread crumbs, salt, and pepper. Spread ^{1}/$_3$ of crumb mixture in bottom of au gratin dish. Cover with half of oysters. Spread ^{1}/$_3$ of crumb mixture over oysters. Cover with remaining oysters. Measure oyster liquor and add enough cream to make 1 cup. Stir in Worcestershire and hot pepper sauce. Pour over oysters. Spread remaining crumb mixture on top and bake 30 minutes or until lightly browned.

Food from Chinatown

We have come a long way from the time when Chow Mein and Chop Suey served in America were considered authentic Chinese food. Fortunately superb, authentic Chinese food is available today and, if the truth be known, I have eaten better Chinese food on Mott Street in Chinatown than in present-day China! Sesame Noodles are Szechuan, easy to make, and so popular they often are served at home as an appetizer or side dish when nothing else on the menu is Chinese.

Cold Sesame Noodles

4 tbsp chicken stock or water
3 tbsp soy sauce
2 tbsp dark sesame oil
1 tbsp each dry sherry and rice or red wine vinegar
3 tbsp sesame paste or creamy peanut butter
1 1/2 tsp sugar
1 tsp chili oil or to taste
1/4 tsp five-spice powder or to taste (optional)
3 cloves garlic, finely minced
2 or 3 scallions, sliced
1 tbsp minced fresh ginger
8 oz Chinese egg noodles or vermicilli, cooked

Process first 9 ingredients in blender until well combined. Stir in garlic, scallions, and ginger. Toss with cooked noodles and serve at room temperature.

Glazed Bananas

Dessert in Chinese restaurants usually is an unimportant part of the meal. Most Chinese restaurants don't offer much beyond a fortune cookie, an occasional kumquat, or a scoop of indifferent ice cream. But, for those in the know, even though you rarely see Glazed or Caramelized Bananas on a menu, you can get them at some restaurants in Chinatown if you ask for them. Ask! They're wonderful.

---

light brown sugar
light corn syrup
I banana per person, cut into chunks
vegetable oil for deep-frying
Ice water

Combine brown sugar and corn syrup in saucepan (I tbsp corn syrup for each 3 tbsp brown sugar). Cook, stirring, until sugar dissolves and mixture thickens. Make enough syrup to coat all chunks of banana. Deep-fry banana chunks in hot oil about 2 minutes or until lightly browned. Dip fried banana into hot syrup with slotted spoon, coating chunks completely. Remove with slotted spoon and insert toothpicks into banana chunks. Place on lightly buttered serving dish. Dip coated chunks into ice water immediately to harden glaze.

Food from Little Italy

There are Italian restaurants all over the city — large and small — good, bad, and indifferent. Some specialize in the cooking of Southern Italy, some of Northern Italy, and some serve both. Little Italy, at the southern end of Manhattan, offers some of the best Italian food in the city. Fettuccine Alfredo is a well-known and popular dish from Northern Italy. It's easy to prepare, but must be made with properly cooked fresh pasta, and other very fresh ingredients. The original version didn't include cream. It was made with a very rich butter not available commercially. If you're counting calories, forget about this dish. Low calorie substitutions for the cream and butter will make this a dish hardly worth eating.

Fettuccine Alfredo

---

1 lb fresh fettuccine, cooked al dente
1/4 lb unsalted butter, melted and still warm
3/4 cup warmed heavy cream
1 cup freshly grated Parmesan cheese
freshly ground pepper to taste

Drain fettuccine but do not rinse. Place in warm bowl, add warm butter, and toss gently. Pour in warmed cream and toss. Add 3/4 cup cheese and pepper to taste. Toss again. Sprinkle remaining cheese on top and serve immediately.

The Magnificent Italian Wedge

Wedges, measured by the foot, are wonderful for informal entertaining. If you have an Italian delicatessen near by, the delicatessen can make a Wedge for you in any length you want. But you can also "construct" one yourself. No cooking is involved, and you can save lots of money.

There's no such thing as an exact and specific recipe for a Wedge. Begin with Italian bread, split down the center lengthwise. Estimate 4 servings per loaf. Cut off ends of bread and spread olive oil generously on inside of both halves of bread with pastry brush. Rub with cut half of garlic. Set top halves of loaves aside and arrange bottom halves end to end on plank or long, heavy piece of cardboard covered with aluminum foil. Select an assortment of different kinds of food from suggestions that follow (or any other food you want to use), and arrange generously on bread. Sprinkle with vinegar and cover with top halves of bread. Cut into serving-size portions.

---

meat (about I lb for each loaf): Genoa, Milano, or Felinetti salami; Prosciutto; Pepperoni; Capicolla; Mortadella; Bresaolo cheese (about ³/₄ lb for each loaf): Provolone; Fontina; Taleggio; Gorgonzola; Mozzarella; Bel Paese
misc: hot peppers; sweet peppers; roasted peppers; anchovies; pickled mushrooms; sliced onion; sliced tomato; lettuce; Italian seasoning.

Chicken Kiev from Russia

The most famous Russian restaurant in New York is the Russian Tea Room, opened in the 1920s. Even the Cold War didn't dim its popularity. Proximity to Carnegie Hall makes this a convenient place to eat before or after a concert. Diners, if they are lucky enough to get a table downstairs (which is very unlikely), can view celebrities, admire the decor, and sample Russian food. Chicken Kiev is a classic Russian dish, not meant for anyone who can't eat real butter.

---

6 tbsp sweet butter, softened
1 tsp each fresh lemon juice and snipped chives
salt and freshly ground pepper to taste
4 large chicken cutlets, pounded to 1/8-inch thickness
1 cup all-purpose flour
1 egg, beaten
1 cup dry bread crumbs
vegetable oil for deep frying

Place butter in bowl, add lemon juice, chives, salt, and pepper. Beat until well combined. Shape into 4 fingers about 3 inches long and place in freezer. Chill until firm. Season chicken cutlets with salt and pepper. Wrap each chicken cutlet around finger of chilled butter, enclosing butter completely. Secure with wooden toothpick if desired. Dip in flour, then egg, then bread crumbs. Refrigerate about 1 hour. Heat oil to 360°F. Deep-fry about 5 minutes. Drain on paper towels and serve immediately.

Tempura from Japan

A quick look at current restaurant guides show there are only a few countries, primarily France, Italy, and China, that have more good restaurants in New York than Japan has. Many serve the ever popular Tempura. It's so popular in Japan that there are wonderful small restaurants where the only food served is Tempura.

Estimate 10 pieces of food per serving, a combination of: jumbo shrimp, shelled and deveined, tails intact; scallops; eggplant, peeled and cut into 1/4-inch wedges; sweet potatoes, peeled and cut into 1/4-inch slices; large mushrooms, cleaned and stems removed; green bell peppers, seeds removed and quartered; flowerettes of cauliflower and broccoli.

Batter (about 1 1/2 cups):
1 egg yolk, beaten
1 cup ice water
1 cup all-purpose flour
Dipping Sauce:
1 cup fish stock (if a Japanese grocery store is available, use dashi)
3 tbsp light soy sauce
1 tbsp sugar
1 tbsp mirin (rice wine)

vegetable oil for deep-frying
flour for dusting
accompaniments: freshly grated ginger and hot white radish

---

somewhat lumpy. Place sauce ingredients in saucepan, stir, bring to a boil, and keep warm. Heat oil in deep-fryer to 360°F. Lightly dust food with flour, dip into batter, and deep-fry a few pieces at a time. Cook about 3 minutes or until lightly browned, turning once. Drain on paper towels and keep warm. Place assortment of cooked food on each plate, pour dipping sauce into small bowls, and serve with small amount of ginger and radish.

Baked French Brie in Puff Pastry

Not surprisingly, there are several very fine French restaurants in New York where you can find French Brie and puff pastry, ingredients for which we can all thank France.

---

1 wheel baby Brie (about 1 lb)
1 sheet (1/2 of 17 1/4 oz pkg) frozen puff pastry,
thawed and rolled out to 14-inch circle
1 jar (10 oz) apricot jam
egg wash for pastry
cocktail crackers to serve

Preheat oven to 375°F. Place Brie on pastry circle and cover with jam. Brush edges of pastry with egg wash and fold pastry up over Brie. Seal edges and place on lined baking sheet. Brush with egg wash and bake 30 minutes.

Pfeffernüsse from Germany

You can buy all kinds of German food in Yorkville, on the upper East Side. But the best-known German restaurant, Lüchow's, opened in 1882, was miles away. It closed a few years ago, leaving behind a history of hearty food in an old-world setting, frequented by a Who's Who of musicians, artists, and politicians. Pfeffernüsse is a traditional Christmas cookie, available freshly baked in German bakeries.

---

4 tbsp butter, room temperature
1 cup firmly packed light brown sugar
3 eggs, beaten
2 tsp grated lemon peel
$1/2$ tsp aniseed
3 cups all-purpose flour
1 tsp each baking soda and cinnamon
$1/2$ tsp each nutmeg and allspice
$1/4$ tsp each salt and freshly ground pepper
confectioners sugar
(makes about 4 dozen cookies)

Cream butter and brown sugar, beat in eggs, and stir in lemon peel and aniseed. Combine remaining ingredients, except confectioners sugar, and stir into egg mixture. Cover and refrigerate overnight. Preheat oven to 375°F. Grease baking sheets. Shape into 1-inch balls and place 1 inch apart on baking sheets. Bake 10 to 12 minutes or until lightly browned. Cool on racks and roll in confectioners sugar.

Index